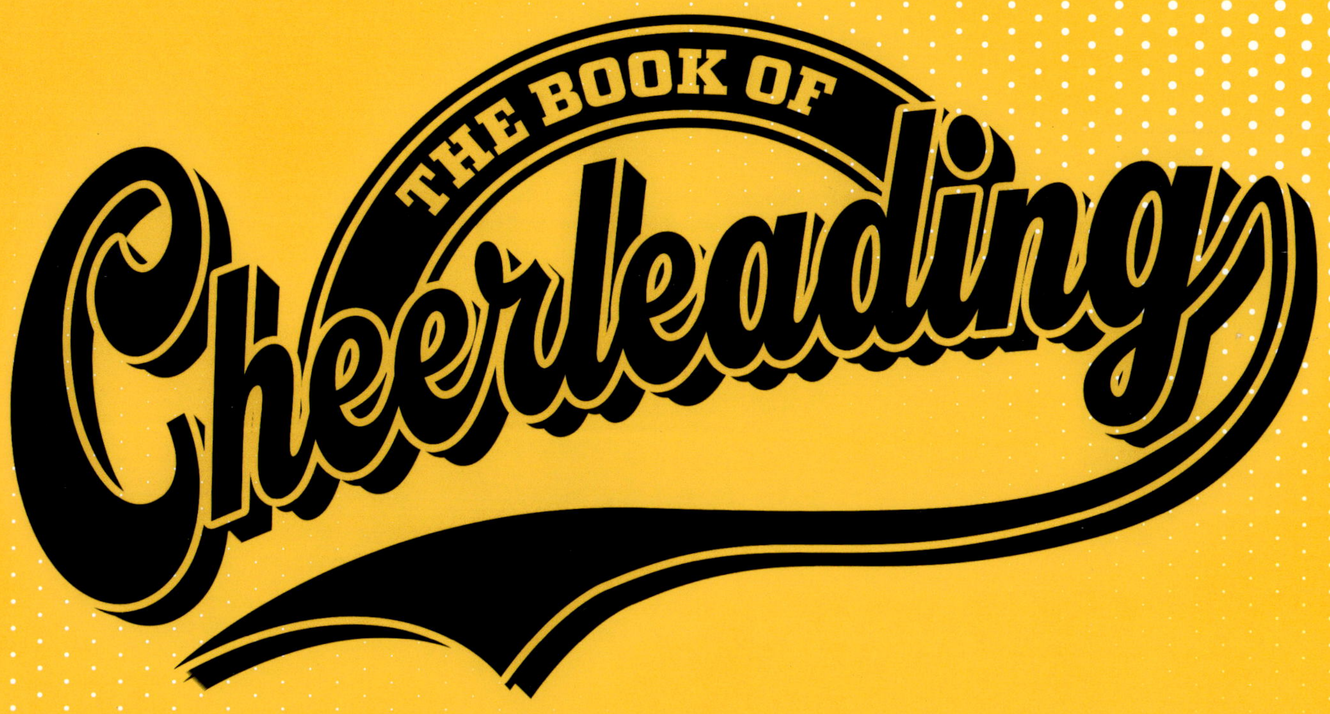

HOW TO BE A CHAMPION CHEERLEADER

First published in the US in 2024
by Welbeck Children's Books
An imprint of Hachette Children's Group

10 9 8 7 6 5 4 3 2

ISBN: 978 1 83935 293 5

Printed in China

This book contains tips on exercise and other activities.
With any new activity, start off gently and build up slowly to avoid injury.

Welbeck Children's Books
An imprint of Hachette Children's Group
Part of Hodder & Stoughton Limited
Carmelite House, 50 Victoria Embankment
London EC4Y 0DZ

An Hachette UK Company
www.hachette.co.uk
www.hachettechildrens.co.uk

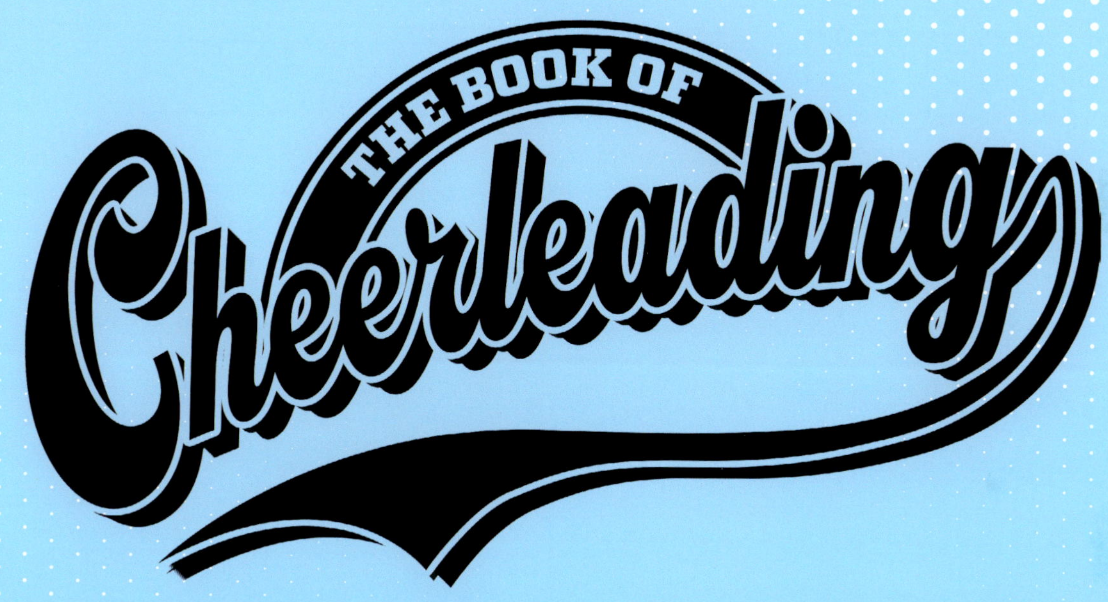

The Book of Cheerleading

HOW TO BE A CHAMPION CHEERLEADER

WELBECK
CHILDREN'S BOOKS

CONTENTS

Go Team!
Welcome to the
fun, fast, and fabulous
world of
CHEERLEADING!

Whether you're already a cheerleader, want to become one, or are just interested in the world of cheer, this book is for you.

Read on to learn about cheerleading's history, culture, moves, gear, and much more. Three cheers for this amazing activity!

WHAT IS CHEERLEADING?

Cheerleading is a team activity that combines elements of dance and acrobatics with shouted phrases, or "cheers."

Traditionally, cheer squads have entertained crowds at sporting events. They do spectacular stunts that pump up the energy level. They also encourage fans to shout and cheer for their team.

In recent years, cheerleading has moved outside of the sports arena. It is now an activity in its own right. It has its own training programs and competitions that are not tied to the sports field.

Cheerleaders can be any age, from toddler to grandparent. They can be male or female. They can be any ethnicity or race. They can have different abilities. Cheerleading really is for EVERYONE!

WHY WE CHEER

Why should you choose cheer? The number one reason: It's FUN! Cheerleading puts you on stage in front of a crowd. It's a chance to be your very best self—and that feels great.

Cheer

WHAT DO WE WANT?
TOUCHDOWN!
WHEN DO WE WANT IT?
RIGHT NOW!

But there are so many other reasons to cheer. Check out these qualities cheerleading can build. Which ones matter to **YOU?**

★ TEAMWORK ★
Work together!

★ PHYSICAL FITNESS ★
Get in shape!

★ SPORTSMANSHIP ★
Great attitude!

★ DISCIPLINE ★
Get it done!

★ SELF-CONFIDENCE ★
You CAN do it!

★ SOCIAL SKILLS ★
Make new friends!

★ DEDICATION ★
Be committed!

★ LEADERSHIP ★
Inspire others!

★ MENTAL TOUGHNESS ★
Mind over matter!

★ WORK ETHIC ★
Hard work pays off!

★ SELF-ESTEEM ★
Love yourself—you're worth it!

ATTITUDE IS EVERYTHING

When you're in front of a crowd, whether at a sports game or a cheer competition, attitude is everything! A cheerleader's job is to be 100 percent "on"—and to make viewers feel the same way.

How do cheerleaders pump up the energy level?

★ **Smile**—A big, bright smile is a cheerleading must, so turn that frown upside-down. Happiness is contagious!

★ **Voice**—Cheerleaders must deliver chants crisply. In practice, they do voice and breathing exercises to help them shout with style.

★ **Enthusiasm**—Sell it! If you want your crowd to catch the energy, you need to feel it and show it. Be in the moment!

★ **Crisp movement**—Sharp, strong movements are eye-catching. They also show that you're putting in your top effort, which gets the crowd on your side.

The WVU cheerleading team does a routine during the second half of an NCAA college football game between the West Virginia Mountaineers and University of Kansas Jayhawks in Morgantown, WV.

★ HISTORY OF Cheerleading ★

Cheerleading got its start on November 2, 1898. A University of Minnesota student, Johnny Campbell, jumped onto the field at a football game and led the crowd in a chant:

Rah, Rah, Rah!
Ski-u-mah, Hoo-Rah! Hoo-Rah!
Varsity! Varsity! Varsity,
Minn-e-So-Tah!

Other students soon joined Johnny on the field. They yelled, danced, and pumped up the crowd—and viewers loved it. Cheerleading was born!

Early cheerleaders were called "yell leaders." They were most common at Ivy League colleges and universities, where they performed at football games. Over time, the practice of cheerleading spread to high schools and communities.

Yell leaders were mostly male until World War II (1939-45). Many young men went off to war during these years. Females filled in, and cheerleading became a mostly female activity. But men are still welcome! Today, about 15 percent of cheerleaders are male.

The cheerleading squad jumps with enthusiasm for their team at Springfield High School in Pennsylvania.

★ MODERN ★ Cheerleading

Today, cheerleading is one of the most popular activities in the world. Check out these fun facts about cheerleading!

- ★ Cheerleading is most popular in the United States. There are nearly 4 million cheerleaders in the U.S. alone.
- ★ There are hundreds of thousands of cheerleaders outside the U.S.
- ★ About 80 percent of American high schools and colleges have cheer squads.
- ★ Football is the most popular sport for cheerleading. Basketball is second.
- ★ Most cheerleaders are in high school.
- ★ About 12 percent of cheerleaders are age 13 or under.

George W. Bush

Did You Know?
Several U.S. Presidents were cheerleaders:

- ⋆ George W. Bush
- ⋆ Ronald Reagan
- ⋆ Dwight D. Eisenhower
- ⋆ Franklin D. Roosevelt

★ HIGH SCHOOL AND COLLEGE ★ Cheerleading

If you like cheering for a team, high school and college cheerleading may be for you! The main job of school cheerleading squads is to support the school's athletic teams.

- ★ School cheer squads stand in front of the home crowd on the game field or court.
- ★ They perform chants. There are choreographed moves that go with the chants.
- ★ Sometimes the cheerleaders urge the crowd to join in. They get everyone shouting!
- ★ Cheer squads may perform dance routines. The music can be live, from a marching band, or recorded, from a speaker.
- ★ Cheerleaders often do handsprings and other gymnastic stunts.
- ★ Cheer squads may work together to make formations, such as pyramids.

Game Day

On game days, many high school cheer squads show their spirit by wearing their cheer uniforms to school. They may participate in **PEP RALLIES** to get everyone excited.

Did You Know?

Many colleges offer scholarships for top cheerleaders. Amounts range from a few hundred dollars per year to full rides (all college expenses paid).

★ ALL STAR ★ Cheerleading

Best of the Best

The top level in All Star cheerleading is called Elite. It is for athletes with strong cheer training and technical ability. These young women and men are ready to compete at the very highest levels.

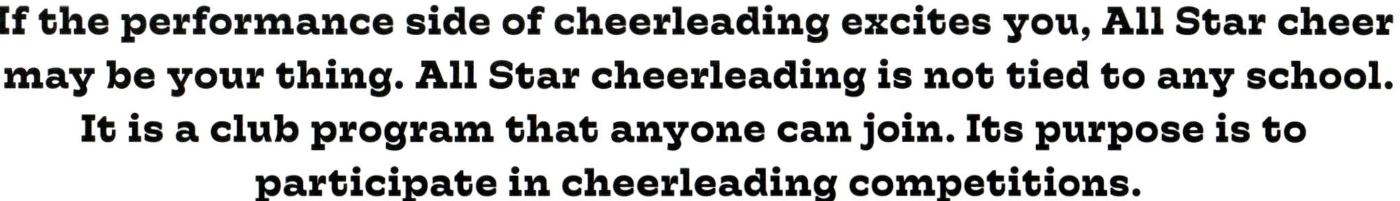

If the performance side of cheerleading excites you, All Star cheer may be your thing. All Star cheerleading is not tied to any school. It is a club program that anyone can join. Its purpose is to participate in cheerleading competitions.

- ★ All Star cheer is open to participants ages 5 to 19.
- ★ There are seven levels, from beginner to advanced.
- ★ Squads learn routines that are two and a half minutes long. The routines are set to recorded music.
- ★ All Star routines consist mostly of acrobatics, formations, and dance moves.
- ★ Chanting and cheering are not usually included in All Star routines.

- ★ A squad usually performs the same routine for a whole year. Most squads enter six to ten competitions per year.
- ★ All Star cheerleading is about energy, energy, energy! The routines are fast and furious.

Did You Know?

All Star cheer has gone international! There are growing programs in the UK, Australia, and even South Korea.

PROFESSIONAL Cheerleading

For some people, cheerleading is a job! Professional cheerleaders work for sports teams. They perform at games to entertain the crowd.

Baltimore Ravens cheerleaders performing during the Super Bowl XXXV Game against the New York Giants in Tampa, Florida.

* Pro cheerleading mostly involves dance routines, not acrobatics or chants.
* Professional cheerleading is usually a part-time job.
* In the United States, five sports have pro cheer leagues: football, basketball, ice hockey, baseball, and soccer.
* Pro cheerleaders are team ambassadors. They don't just cheer—they have to attend community events, too.

Top Squad!

In the world of pro cheerleading, the Dallas Cowboys Cheerleaders are at the top of the pyramid. This all-female team is probably the world's best known cheer squad.

Cheer

WATCH US JUMP!
WATCH US ROCK!
WE'RE THE SQUAD THAT
CAN'T BE STOPPED!

Did You Know?

Most professional cheerleaders have a strong dance background, not just cheerleading experience.

INTERNATIONAL CHEERLEADING

Canada

United States

Mexico

Top Tier

After the U.S., Canada and Mexico are the top two countries for cheer. But China, Australia, Japan, and the UK are coming on strong!

Cheerleading may be an American invention, but it has spread around the world. Today, cheer is popular in many countries outside the U.S. Check out the dots on the map. These countries have official cheer programs! RAH, RAH!

CHEERLEADING POSTITIONS

Every cheerleading team is divided into three main positions: BASE, BACK SPOT (also called spotter), and FLYER.

BASE

This position is at the bottom of any formations. Bases need to be strong and steady! Their job is to lift and hold the flyer. They get their lifting power from their legs, not their arms and backs, which could lead to muscle strains or other injuries.

BACK SPOT

Back spots steady the formation by helping the bases. They call out instructions or keep a verbal count to help everyone keep their rhythm. They also keep an eye on everything to help the flyer keep their balance—and catch them if they fall.

FLYER

Flyers are lifted and thrown in stunts during a routine. They have to make perfect jumps, flips, and spins. Sometimes they strike difficult poses while being held aloft. Flyers must have enormous trust in their squad mates' abilities.

FLYERS are usually the smallest and lightest—and the bravest!

BASES are usually the biggest and strongest members of the squad.

TUMBLING

Tumbling is a form of gymnastics where athletes twist, flip, jump, and roll. It is a cheerleading staple. Tumbling is fun for the crowd to watch—and it's even more fun for the cheerleaders to perform!

Cheer

PUMP, PUMP, PUMP IT UP!
KEEP, KEEP, KEEP IT UP!
TEAM SPIRIT!

Every cheerleader should master three basic moves:

The Handstand

In this move, athletes balance on their hands with their feet in their air. This move is the gateway to more complicated types of tumbling.

The Cartwheel

A cartwheel is basically a rolling handstand, with the legs rotating up and over.

The Back Bend

From a standing position, raise the arms. Bend backward until your hands hit the ground and your body is positioned in an arch.

Level Up!

The **back handspring** is a cheerleading favorite. Do a leaping back bend to land on your hands, then whip the legs up and over the head to land on your feet. This move is a show stopper!

CHEERS

They're named CHEERleaders because they lead CHEERS! Cheers get the crowd involved. Check out these fun cheer types.

TEAM PRIDE CHEERS

WE'VE GOT SPIRIT,
YES WE DO!
WE'VE GOT SPIRIT,
HOW 'BOUT YOU?

CROWD RESPONSE CHEERS

WHEN WE SAY LIONS,
YOU SAY ROAR!
CHEERLEADERS: **LIONS!**
CROWD: **ROAR!**

DEFENSE & OFFENSE CHEERS

SCORE! SCORE!
WE WANT MORE!
A TISKET, A TASKET,
BLOCK THAT BASKET!

SPELLING CHEERS

GIVE ME A G!
GIVE ME AN O!
WHAT'S IT SPELL?
GO! GO TEAM!

VICTORY CHEERS

VICTORY'S OURS!
WE'RE THE STARS!

Ways to Get Loud

- Do exercises to strengthen your diaphragm (the muscle that controls your breathing).
- Practice yawning to open up the back of your throat.
- Concentrate on good pronunciation. This improves your voice quality.
- Practice shouting while doing cardio. Build your vocal endurance!
- Speak in a lower tone than usual. This will make you louder.

ARM MOTIONS

Simple arm motions are the most basic cheerleading moves. You'll use them in every routine! Here are the five most common motions.

Clasp

The classic cheerleading clap. It ends with the hands clasped at the chin and the elbows at the sides.

T-Motion

The arms stick straight out to the sides so the body forms a T shape. The fists are clenched, with the fingers pointing downward.

High V

The arms are lifted in a V shape, with the fists clenched and the fingers pointing outward.

Cone

A variation on the touchdown motion, with the hands clasped instead of separate.

Touchdown

The arms are held up like a football referee calling a touchdown, with the hands curled into fists.

Lots to Learn

There are dozens of common arm motions in cheerleading. Every squad has its favorites. Cheerleaders do drills, practicing the motions over and over until they become second nature.

Cheer

PASS...THE BALL!
PASS, PASS THE BALL!
WIN...IT ALL!
WIN, WIN IT ALL!

JUMPS

Cheerleaders jump during routines. Sometimes they jump in between cheers, too—just because they're feeling the energy, and they want to jump for joy! Try these common jumps on for size.

Spread Eagle

This one is super simple. Just leap up and extend the arms and legs into an X shape.

Toe Touch

The arms are in a T position and the legs are straddled.

Hurdler

The arms are in a T position. One leg extends forward and the other is bent backward.

Pike

The arms and legs are both extended forward.

Herkie

Similar to the Hurdler, but the bent leg is lower down.

Cheer

PUMP, PUMP, PUMP IT UP!
JUMP, JUMP, JUMP IT UP!
KEEP, KEEP, KEEP IT UP!
TEAM SPIRIT!

Did You Know?

The **herkie** is named after Lawrence Herkimer, a former cheerleader and the founder of the National Cheerleaders Association. It is one of the most common cheer moves.

STUNTS

Cheerleaders work together to pull off exciting stunts and wow the crowd! They put lots of basic moves and positions together to create spectacular displays of skill. Check out a few basic stunts.

Cheer

GIVE US A W!
GIVE US AN I!
GIVE US AN N!
WIN! WIN! WIN!

Liberty

The flyer balances on one leg on the base's hands. The arms and the other leg are raised. An experienced cheerleader may strike harder poses. For instance, they may raise one leg vertically above their head.

Pyramids

Pyramids are group formations, with different cheerleaders doing different things. There are endless ways to do pyramids. They are limited only by the squad's creativity, imagination, and skill!

Basket Toss

The flyer is tossed into the air. The other cheerleaders interweave their arms to form a basket and catch her on the way down.

CHEER ROUTINES

School cheer squads often work routines into their gameday performances. Routines are carefully choreographed and practiced in advance.

Some routines are short, lasting just five or ten seconds and accompanying a specific music clip. Short routines are often performed during time-outs or other brief stoppages. They are typically gameday staples that a squad uses over and over at every event.

Some routines are longer. They might be performed at halftime. Longer routines are usually specially choreographed for a single use.

Routines might include:

★ **CHEERS** Stand and shout!

★ **TUMBLING** This is a time for the squad's amazing acrobats to shine!

★ **DANCE** Pump up the volume and boogie down!

★ **LIFTS** Simple lifts and positions are a sideline staple.

★ **PYRAMIDS** Most common during extended breaks in the game, when there is more time to work.

Cheerleaders perform for an NFL game at Inglewood, California 2012.

CHEERLEADING COMPETITIONS

Who's the best? There's only one way to find out. Let's go head-to-head and compete!

International Cheerleading Championships
Vancouver, Canada 2017

Cheer

**BIG "G"
LITTLE "O"
WHAT'S IT SPELL?
GO, GO, GO!**

COMPETITION TYPES

Sometimes school cheerleading squads compete against each other. Competitions can include squads from many local schools.

All Star cheerleaders (who do not cheer for any school) only do organized competitions. They do not do any gametime cheering.

COUNTDOWN: 00:02:30

Competition routines cannot exceed two and a half minutes. Most squads choreograph their routines to music so they can plan them right down to the second. They want every bit of time available to show their winning stuff!

The National High School Cheerleading Championship (NHSCC) is America's biggest high school cheer competition. The 2023 event hosted 1,125 teams from 33 states. One of the competition's events, Game Day Live, allows cheer squads to perform with their school marching bands.

CHEERLEADING WORLDS

The Cheerleading World Championships, known as "Worlds," is an international competition held every spring in Orlando, Florida. It is the biggest event of the year for All Star squads. Only the top teams receive an invitation, or "bid," to compete at Worlds.

2023 WORLDS

PARTICIPANTS: 11,590
TEAMS: 539
COUNTRIES: 18

Judging Categories:

- Stunts
- Pyramids
- Tosses
- Creativity
- Tumbling
- Jumps
- Dance
- Routine Composition
- Performance

Hitting Zero

Judges take off points for mistakes. Performing a routine without getting any deductions is called "**hitting zero**." It is the gold standard!

Did You Know?

There are 22 divisions in Worlds. All athletes from all winning teams receive a championship ring!

2022 Cheerleading Worlds

IS CHEERLEADING A SPORT?

Every cheerleader knows the answer to this question:

YES!!!

March 19, 2015: Kentucky Wildcats male cheerleaders perform during a second-round NCAA Tournament game between the Hampton University Pirates and the University of Kentucky Wildcats at the KFC Yum! Center in Louisville, KY.

Cheerleading requires intense athletic ability, long hours of practice, and teamwork. Cheer squads compete with each other, just like other sports teams do.

The NCAA (National College Athletic Association) and other sports regulating bodies in the United States do not yet recognize cheerleading as a sport.

In 2021, however, the International Olympic Committee did recognize cheerleading as a sport. This means cheer could show up in the Olympics...possibly as soon as 2028. Stay tuned for exciting developments on this front!

Cheer

MAKE SOME NOISE!
HELP US OUT!
RAISE YOUR VOICE!
HEAR US SHOUT!
V-I-C-T-O-R-Y!

Did You Know?

Over 90 percent of all female cheerleaders have some gymnastics experience. Among male cheerleaders, the figure is closer to 20 percent.

STUNT

STUNT is a new type of cheer competition for females only. It lets participants show off their skills while meeting the requirements to be an "official" sport.

In **STUNT**, cheerleading teams compete at the same time on a game field, performing identical moves. The team that does the best job wins.

A STUNT game has four quarters, each with a different theme:

1. **Partner Stunts**
2. **Pyramids and Tosses**
3. **Jumps and Tumbling**
4. **Team Routines**

During the fourth quarter, finalists perform routines that combine elements from the first three quarters.

NCAA Divisions I, II, and III have all expressed support for acknowledging STUNT as a sport. The official decision has not yet been made. But official or not, STUNT is growing fast. More than 60 U.S. colleges now have STUNT squads—and the number is sure to increase!

Did You Know?

STUNT has three separate divisions: college, high school, and club. The club division is open to athletes between 5 and 25 years of age.

CHEER GEAR

It's game day! Grab your stuff. What gear will you need to cheer your team to victory?

Pom-poms

Pom-poms are balls made of shiny streamers, with plastic handles for easy grip. "Poms" add sparkle and flash to any event!

Signs

Do you need to spell out a word for the crowd? How about share a team spirit message? Signs act as a visual aid to get your point across.

Megaphone

Shout into the narrow end. Big noise comes out the wide end! Megaphones amplify sound, letting cheerleaders' chants be heard.

Flags

Waving, swooping flags are colorful and eye-catching. Work them into your routine for a show-stopping effect!

What's in the Bag?

What's in YOUR cheer bag? Check out these must-have items.

Sunscreen

Water bottle

Snacks

Hairbrush

Athletic tape

Change of clothes

Deodorant

Sweat towel

Extra hair ties

UNIFORMS

Cheer squads wear colorful, matching uniforms that provide style and flair!

Accessorize!

Don't forget the accessories! Big, cute hair bows are a must. Fun accents like nail polish, bright lipstick, and temporary tattoos can level up your look.

School cheer uniforms usually bear the school's colors and logo. All-Star uniforms tend to be flashier and made of flexible fabrics such as Lycra and spandex.

- **TOPS** are form fitting. Some tops go all the way to the waist. Others are crop tops that show part of the cheerleader's stomach.
- **SHIRTS** can be sleeveless, long sleeved, or anything in between.
- **SKIRTS** are often pleated. In high school and college cheer, they are usually mid thigh length. Some cheer squads wear SHORTS. Shorts are very common in pro cheerleading.

- **CHEER BRIEFS** are a bit like swimsuit bottoms. They are worn under the skirt and they are designed to be seen—they are not underwear!
- Some cheer uniforms are short **DRESSES** instead of top/bottom combos.

Male cheerleaders wear looser shirts and shorts or stretchy pants.

PRACTICE TIME

Like any team, a cheerleading squad needs to practice.

Cheer

WHAT WE GOT?
WHAT WE GOT?
WE GOT A TEAM THAT'S
HOT, HOT, HOT!

A typical cheer practice is about two hours long and might be divided up like this:

- **Warm-Up** – 10 minutes
- **Tumbling Foundations** – 15 minutes
- **Take-Off & Landing Drills** – 10 minutes
- **Tumbling Skills** – 20 minutes
- **Stunting** – 20 minutes
- **Conditioning** – 20 minutes
- **Flexibility Training** – 15 minutes
- **Routine /Choreography** – 10 minutes

That's not a lot of time for each skill. You can see why a good squad needs to meet OFTEN to polish their performance!

A Big Commitment?

The number of practices per week depends a lot on a squad's level. Highly skilled squads may practice most days. More casual squads might meet once or twice a week—just enough to learn the basics.

School squads will attend games and competitions on top of their practice hours. All Star squads don't have games, but they will travel regularly to competitions. They usually practice more often than school squads.

COACHING THE TEAM

Every cheerleading squad has a hidden but essential member: the COACH!

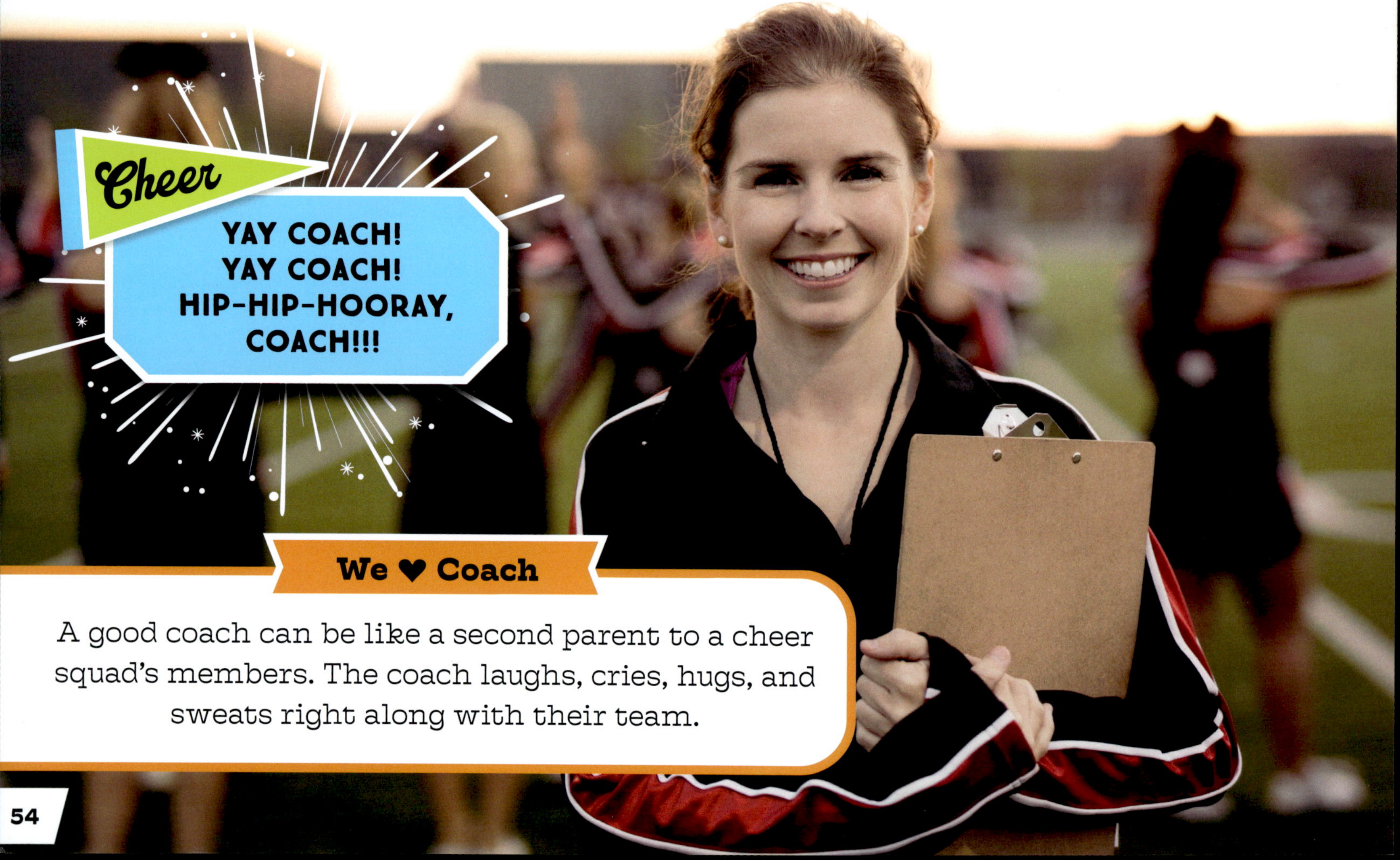

Cheer

YAY COACH!
YAY COACH!
HIP-HIP-HOORAY, COACH!!!

We ♥ Coach

A good coach can be like a second parent to a cheer squad's members. The coach laughs, cries, hugs, and sweats right along with their team.

The coach is the person who manages every aspect of the cheer squad. Here are a few of the things the coach does:

- **KEEP** a master schedule
- **PLAN** practices
- **CHOREOGRAPH** routines
- **TEACH** stunts, tumbling, and other skills
- **SUPERVISE** strength and flexibility training
- **INSPIRE** and **NURTURE** athletes
- **ORGANIZE** travel to games and competitions
- **MANAGE** dues and other money
- **ORDER** equipment and uniforms
- **COMMUNICATE** with parents

It's a lot of work...but it's a labor of love. Most coaches are former cheerleaders themselves. Coaching lets them remain part of the cheer world while passing their hard-earned skills to a new generation.

CHEER STRONG

Do you think cheerleaders just hop around on the field, looking great? Think again! Cheerleading is an intensely physical activity that puts all of a body's muscles to work. Let's take a look.

Strength Training

To build their arm and leg muscles, cheerleaders do strength training during practice, such as lifting weights.

- To strengthen their core, cheerleaders do sit-ups, planks, and yoga.
- To prime their heart and lungs, cheerleaders do cardio machines or other high-intensity exercise, such as running.

ARMS

- Constantly in motion during cheers
- Used to lift and steady other cheerleaders
- Used during tumbling and other stunts

HEART and LUNGS

Work hard to supply the body with blood and oxygen during physical activity

CORE

- Essential for balance during formations
- Used during tumbling and other stunts

LEGS

- Cheerleaders are always on their feet!
- Used for lifting power
- Used during tumbling and other stunts

BEND AND STRETCH

Cheerleaders twist and turn their bodies in ways that most people don't. They need to be flexible to perform at their peak.

Why is flexibility so important in cheer? Let's talk about a few reasons:

- **Gymnastics.** Tumbles and flips—enough said! Flexible joints are needed for handsprings, cartwheels, and other sideline staples.
- **Poses.** How about the scorpion—you know, the one with the leg above the head? Try THAT one without flexibility.
- **Blood flow.** Flexibility increases blood flow throughout your body, which improves your physical performance.
- **Injury protection.** The more flexible you are, the less prone you are to injury.
- **Relaxation.** Stretching is relaxing and improves your mental well-being—and that's good for everyone, cheerleader or not!

Try Yoga

Yoga is a great way to improve your flexibility and have fun at the same time. Why not make it a team activity?

Remember to speak to a physician before starting any new fitness program.

SAFETY MATTERS

With its spectacular stunts and tosses, cheerleading is amazing to watch—but it can also be dangerous.

Cheer

**HEY, CROWD!
SAY IT LOUD!
SAY IT PROUD!
GO TEAM!**

If flyers fall, they can be seriously injured. Tumblers can give themselves strains and sprains. Pyramids can collapse, leading to concussions, bruises, and even broken bones.

In the early 2000s, cheerleading was the number one most dangerous activity for female athletes. But cheer organizations have gotten much more serious about safety, and it shows. From 2012 to the present, there have been only three catastrophic injuries in US cheerleading.

What steps do cheer squads take to stay safe? Here are a few.

- **Floor mats:** Cushioning floor mats are used during practice and sometimes performance to break falls.
- **Strength and flexibility training:** Strong, flexible athletes are less prone to injury.
- **Coach certification:** Cheerleading safety certification teaches coaches to use safe practices.
- **Spotters:** Spotters are required for pyramids and basket tosses, both in practice and competition.
- **Restrictions:** Restrictions on stunts make them safer. For example, pyramids cannot be more than two person heights (in high school) or two and a half person heights (in college). Flyers must keep a head-up position during a toss.
- **Safe surfaces:** Stunts should not be performed on slippery grass or other unsafe surfaces.

MAKING THE SQUAD

So you're sold on cheerleading. You want to give it a try. GREAT! There's just one little thing: You have to make the squad. How do you do it?

Well, it depends. Are you going for a school squad or All Star?

SCHOOL CHEER

To earn a place on a high school or college squad, you'll have to try out.

★ A tryout is like an audition. You'll perform for the coach and probably a few squad members.

★ They'll judge your skills, attitude, and overall presentation.

★ They might look at your grades, too. If they like what they see...you're in!

ALL STAR CHEER

All Star cheer is for everyone. This means that when you go All Star, it's not really a question of "yes" or "no," it's about finding your fit.

★ You'll probably attend a few practices.

★ Coaches will evaluate your skills.

★ Then they'll tell you where you belong...for now. Work hard, though, and you're sure to move up quickly!

If you don't make the squad on your first try, don't get discouraged! Work on your skills and try again. It's never too late to cheer!

CHEER CAMPS

Summer's here...break from cheer? No way! Summer vacation is the perfect time to attend cheer camp. Ranging in duration from a few days to over a week, cheer camps let you immerse yourself in all things cheer.

WHAT TO EXPECT

What happens at cheer camp? Here are some things to expect.

- **Make new friends:** You'll make all kinds of new pals at cheer camp.
- **Team bonding:** If you go with your team, you'll all know each other MUCH better by the end of cheer camp—trust us!
- **Exhaustion:** Cheer camp is a LOT of work and you'll be tired...but it's worth it!

WHO ATTENDS CHEER CAMP?

Individual cheerleaders (both male and female) can attend cheer camp. Whole squads and their coaches often attend as well.

- **Learning:** Work on your skills and routines.
- **Sleepovers:** Every night is a sleepover with your besties—what could be better than that?
- **Eating, eating, eating:** You'll be starving after every day of hard work. Endless buffets will cure your hunger pangs!

INCLUSION IN CHEER

Cheer is for everyone, and lots of organizations are working to make sure this activity is open to all participants.

Check out some of the inclusion initiatives in the cheer world today.

Racial Diversity: Organizations such as Black Girls Cheer work to ensure that people of all races and ethnicities are represented in cheer.

Special Olympics: USA Cheer (the governing body for cheerleading in the US) has teamed up with the Special Olympics to bring cheer to people of all abilities. Special Olympics teams can be Traditional (100 percent with intellectual disabilities) or Unified (50 percent or more with intellectual disabilities).

Professional Guys: In 2019, men cheered professionally in the US National Football League (NFL) for the first time, when the Los Angeles Rams welcomed cheerleaders Quinton Peron and Napoleon Jinnies to the squad.

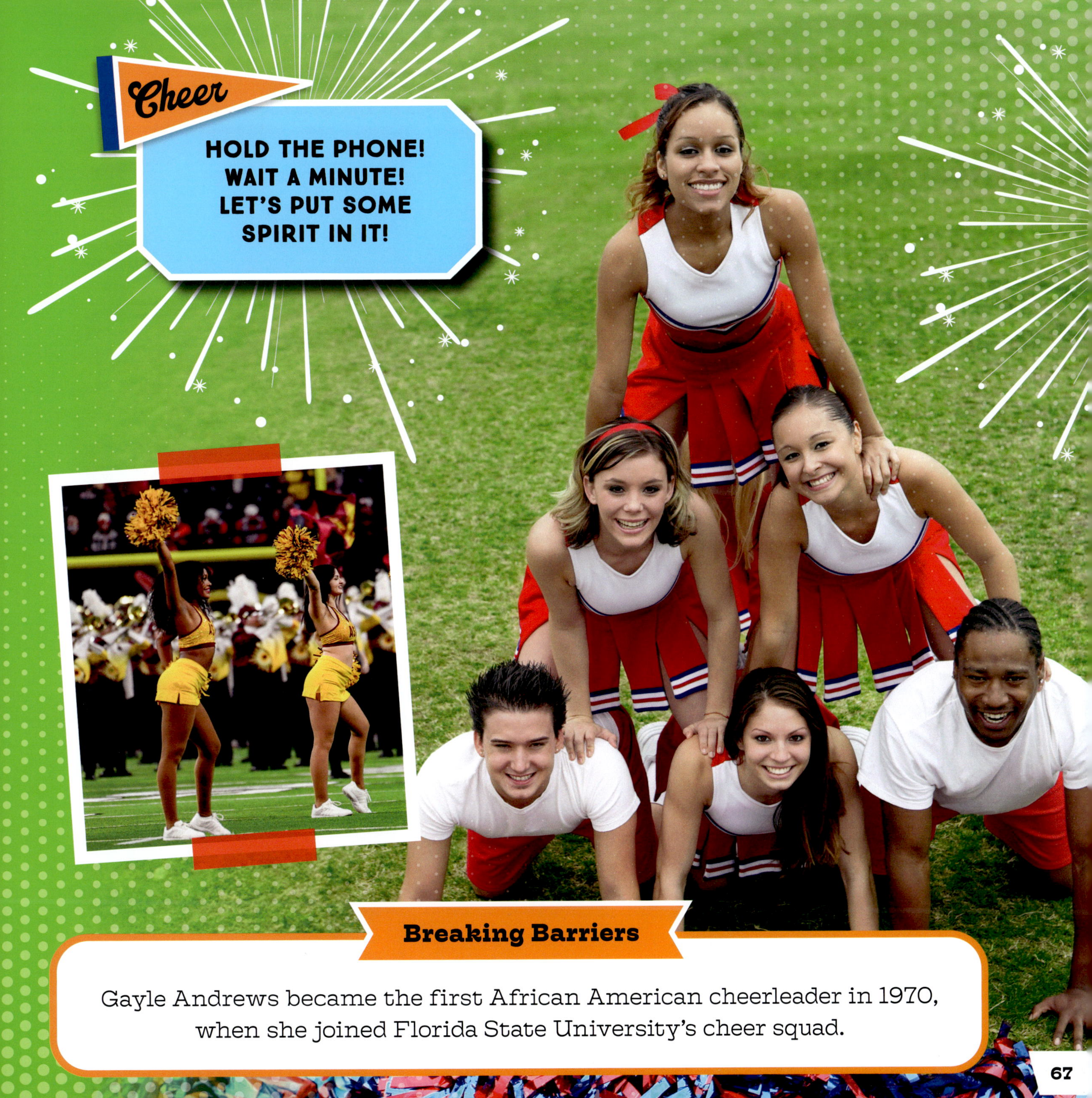

Breaking Barriers

Gayle Andrews became the first African American cheerleader in 1970, when she joined Florida State University's cheer squad.

Cheer LEADING!

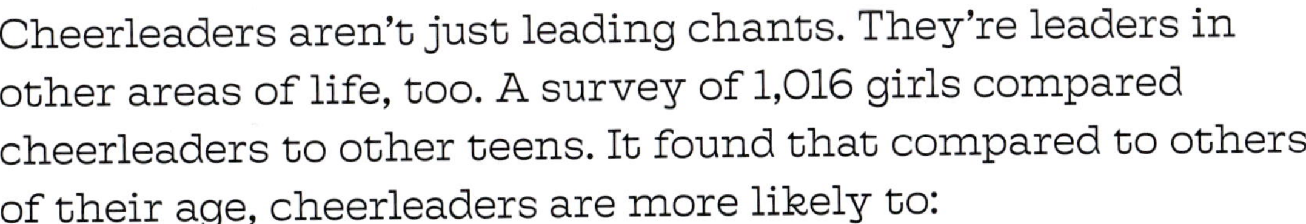

Cheerleaders aren't just leading chants. They're leaders in other areas of life, too. A survey of 1,016 girls compared cheerleaders to other teens. It found that compared to others of their age, cheerleaders are more likely to:

- ★ **Volunteer their time (56% vs. 46%)**
- ★ **Join an organization at school (43% vs. 24%)**
- ★ **Hold a leadership position in or out of school (57% vs. 46%)**
- ★ **Participate in Student Council (33% vs. 25%)**

Also, 81% of cheerleaders held a grade point average of 3.5 or higher—that's good stuff!

Groups Doing Good

Some middle and high school cheer squads have community service days where they volunteer as a group. For example, they might clean up a park, collect school supplies, or help out at events. Service days are a great way to show that winning cheer spirit, do some good, and have fun at the same time!

GLOSSARY

All Star cheer: Cheerleading performed as a club rather than a school activity, with competition as the ultimate goal.

back spot: A position behind the formation that steadies the other participants and catches the flyer if anything goes wrong.

base: A position at the base of formations that lifts and holds the flyer.

cheer: A chant performed in front of a crowd to pump up energy levels and support a sports team.

choreograph: To plan the combination of moves, stunts, and chants that will make up a cheer routine.

coach: The person who plans a cheer squad's activities and teaches and trains its members.

drills: Practices that repeat a certain skill over and over.

flexibility: The ability to bend and stretch easily.

flyer: A cheerleader who is thrown and lifted during stunts.

formation: The arrangement of a squad. May refer to standing positions on the field or positions during a stunt.

inclusion: Providing equal access to people of all races, ethnicities, and abilities.

jumps: Cheerleading moves that involve leaping off the ground.

lifts: Any cheerleading moves that involve lifting someone off the ground.

megaphone: An amplifying device. A cheerleader shouts into the small end, and a louder noise comes out the wide end.

pep rally: An energetic pregame gathering designed to boost team spirit.

pom-poms: Balls made of shiny streamers, with plastic handles for easy grip. Often waved during cheer routines.

routine: A choreographed set of moves and/or chants.

sport: An activity involving physical exertion for the purpose of competition within an official sponsoring organization or school.

squad: The group of athletes that makes up a cheerleading unit.

STUNT: A sport-style cheerleading competition performed on a playing field by two opposing cheer squads.

stunts: Also called pyramid building, stunts involve multiple cheerleaders working together to build formations.

tumbling: A form of gymnastics in which athletes use their bodies to twist, roll, flip, and jump.

uniform: Matching clothing worn by all members of a cheer squad.

Worlds: Short for Cheerleading World Championships, the most important All Star competition each year.

CREDITS

The publishers would like to thank the following sources for their kind permission to reproduce the pictures in this book.

Alamy: Associated Press 13, 44; /Associated Press/Julio Cortez 66; /Cal Sport Media 41 (bottom), 49 (right); /Hero Images Inc 31 (top), 47 (bottom), 54; /Evan Hurd 41 (top); /Indiana Stock 17; /Brooks Kraft LLC/Sygma 17; /Kirby Lee 18, 39, 67 (left); /Jacek Makowicz 9, 20, 53; /MBI 64-65; /Cathyrose Melloan 19; /Victoria Snowber 49; /Ozkan Ozmen 28; /WoodysPhotos 29 (top right and bottom); /Xinhua 40; /Zoonar GmbH 9, 33

Bridgeman Images: Ewing Galloway/UIG 14; /Photo © Underwood Archives 15

Eunderwoood25: 43

Getty Images: Bettmann 15 (bottom); /clu 32 (left); /James Dawson/WireImage 50, 55; /Digital Vision 67, 68; /franckreporter 7(middle left), 32 (right); /Seth Goldfarb 33 (top right); /Gravity Images 33 (bottom left); /Wesley Hitt 35; /Catherine Ledner 29 (top centre); /Leeznow 7 (top); /Andy Lyons/Allsport 22; /Chris McDill/Icon Sportswire 29 (top left); /JakeOlimb 35; /Mike Powell 7 (right), 8 (left), 34 (left); / rbs1_85 34 (right); /Rubberball Productions-Nicole Hill Gerulat (top right); /George Shelly 35 (top left)

iStockphoto.com: FatCamera 12; /IPGGutenberg 8 (right), 51 (left); /Jmichl 35 (bottom); /Lokibaho 27; /nazarethman 16; /nullplus 48; /Pannarai Nak-im 48; / RichVintage 31 (bottom); /stevecoleimages 11

Shutterstock: Chen WS 47; /Chris Curtis 57; /Di Studio 59; /Hero Images on Offset 61, 62; /mooninblack 51; /Pavel L Photo and Video 21, 45

Every effort has been made to acknowledge correctly and contact the source and/ or copyright holder of each picture. Any unintentional errors or omissions, which will be corrected in future editions of this book.